W9-CBZ-233

Pebble™

First Biographies
Dr. Seuss

USA
37
THEODOR SEUSS GEISEL
2004

by Cheryl Carlson

Consulting Editor: Gail Saunders-Smith, PhD

Capstone
press
Mankato, Minnesota

Pebble Books are published by Capstone Press,
151 Good Counsel Drive, P.O. Box 669, Mankato, Minnesota 56002.
www.capstonepress.com

1 2 3 4 5 6 10 09 08 07 06 05

Library of Congress Cataloging-in-Publication Data
Carlson, Cheryl.
    Dr. Seuss / by Cheryl Carlson
    p. cm.—(First biographies)
    Includes bibliographical references and index.
    ISBN 0-7368-3639-X (hardcover)
    1. Seuss, Dr.—Juvenile literature. 2. Authors, American—20th century—
Biography—Juvenile literature. 3. Illustrators—United States—Biography—Juvenile
literature. 4. Children's literature—Authorship—Juvenile literature. I. Title. II. First
biographies (Mankato, Minn.)
PS3513.E2Z623 2005
813'.52—dc22   2004011904

Summary: Simple text and photographs present the life of Dr. Seuss.

Note to Parents and Teachers

The First Biographies set supports national history standards
for units on people and culture. This book describes and illustrates
the life of Dr. Seuss. The images support early readers in
understanding the text. The repetition of words and phrases helps
early readers learn new words. This book also introduces early
readers to subject-specific vocabulary words, which are defined in
the Glossary section. Early readers may need assistance to read
some words and to use the Table of Contents, Glossary, Read More,
Internet Sites, and Index sections of the book.

Table of Contents

Time Line

1904
born

Early Years

Dr. Seuss was born in 1904 in Massachusetts. His real name was Theodor Seuss Geisel.

◀ childhood home in Springfield, Massachusetts

Time Line

1904
born

1920
graduates from
high school

As a child, Dr. Seuss liked to read. He graduated from high school in 1920. He worked on a magazine. Then he went to college in England.

Springfield High School; yearbook picture of Dr. Seuss (inset)

Time Line

1904
born

1920
graduates from
high school

1937
writes first book

Writing and Drawing

After college, Dr. Seuss
made money drawing.
He had his own studio.
Dr. Seuss wrote and
illustrated his first book
in 1937.

Time Line

1904
born

1920
graduates from
high school

1937
writes first book

In 1957, Dr. Seuss wrote *The Cat in the Hat.* The book used rhymes to tell the story of a silly cat. Dr. Seuss drew funny pictures for the book.

1957
writes *The Cat in the Hat*

Time Line

1904
born

1920
graduates from
high school

1937
writes first book

Many children loved
the stories and drawings
by Dr. Seuss. Some of
his books were made
into movies.

1957
writes *The Cat
in the Hat*

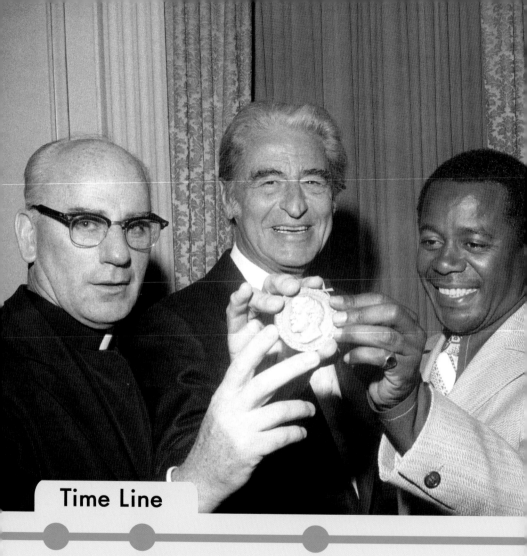

Time Line

1904
born

1920
graduates from
high school

1937
writes first book

Adults also liked stories
and drawings by Dr. Seuss.
He won many awards
for his books and movies.

◀ Dr. Seuss (center) holds one of his awards

1957
writes *The Cat
in the Hat*

Time Line

1904	1920	1937
born	graduates from high school	writes first book

Dr. Seuss wrote and illustrated 44 books during his lifetime. He died in 1991.

1957
writes *The Cat in the Hat*

1991
dies

Time Line

1904
born

1920
graduates from
high school

1937
writes first book

Remembering Dr. Seuss

A library in California is named after Dr. Seuss. People can see a statue of him at the library.

1957
writes *The Cat in the Hat*

1991
dies

Time Line

1904
born

1920
graduates from
high school

1937
writes first book

In 2004, a Hollywood Star
was named for Dr. Seuss.
Today, people still read
and love books that
Dr. Seuss wrote.

1957
writes *The Cat in the Hat*

1991
dies

2004
receives Hollywood Star

Glossary

award—a prize; Dr. Seuss won a Peabody Award, a Pulitzer Prize, an Academy Award, and many others.

college—a place where people study after high school

illustrate—to draw pictures for books

library—a place where books, magazines, newspapers, and other materials are kept for reading and borrowing

rhyme—words that end with the same sound; poems and stories sometimes use rhyme.

studio—a room or building where an artist works

Read More

Adil, Janeen R. *Dr. Seuss.* A Robbie Reader. Hockessin, Del.: Mitchell Lane, 2004.

Lynch, Wendy. *Dr. Seuss.* Lives and Times. Chicago: Heinemann Library, 2000.

Rau, Dana Meachen. *Dr. Seuss.* Rookie Biography. New York: Children's Press, 2003.

Internet Sites

FactHound offers a safe, fun way to find Internet sites related to this book. All of the sites on FactHound have been researched by our staff.

Here's how:

1. Visit *www.facthound.com*
2. Type in this special code **073683639X** for age-appropriate sites. Or enter a search word related to this book for a more general search.
3. Click on the **Fetch It** button.

FactHound will fetch the best sites for you!

Index

Word Count: 184
Grade: 1
Early-Intervention Level: 16

Editorial Credits
Sarah L. Schuette, editor; Heather Kindseth, set designer; Patrick D. Dentinger, book
    designer; Kelly Garvin, photo researcher; Scott Thoms, photo editor

Photo Credits
AP/Wide World Photos, cover; Lenny Ignelzi, 18; Reed Saxon, 20
Corbis/Bettmann, 14; James L. Amos, 16
Courtesy of the Connecticut Valley Historical Museum, Springfield, Massachusetts, 4,
    6 (inset)
Getty Images Inc./Gene Lester, 8, 10, 12
Library of Congress, 6 (main)
US Postal Service, 1

J B SEUSS
Carlson, Cheryl.
Dr. Seuss /